CHURCH EXTENSIONS
AND
ADAPTATIONS

Church House Publishing
Church House, Great Smith Street, London SW1P 3NZ

ISBN 0 7151 7567 X

Published 1996 for the Council for the Care of Churches by Church House Publishing

Printed in England by Longdunn Press Ltd, Bristol

Cover photograph: All Saints, Stock, in the Diocese of Chelmsford, extension on N side (see also page 55).

Contents

Preface

The origins of this book lie in a residential meeting of the Council for the Care of Churches in March 1992 to consider its strategy for the years up to 2000, which are the years of the Decade of Evangelism. We recognised the need to explain to people, both inside the Church and outside, why parishes wish to embark on the demanding and expensive task of adapting their church buildings. We also wanted to offer parishes practical hints on how to go about their task. The preparation of the text was delayed not just by the Bishopsgate bomb which damaged our offices in London Wall, but by the preparation of the report *Mission in Mortar,* which set out in broad terms the Council's affirmation of the positive role buildings can play in furthering the worship and mission of the Church today. This was submitted to the General Synod for debate in July 1993 and found a general welcome. However, some critics complained that the report was too theoretical and did not offer sufficient practical guidance. This book attempts to answer those concerns.

We are grateful to our authors, Jonathan Bailey, William Hawkes, Jonathan MacKechnie-Jarvis and Michael Perham, to Christopher Dalton who supplied all the photographs, and to the staff at the Council and at Church House Publishing who edited and produced the book.

Rt Revd Colin Scott
Bishop of Hulme
Chairman of the Council for the Care of Churches

St Matthew, Salford Priors, Coventry Diocese: glazed metal screen to meeting room.

Introduction

The Council has been considering for some time whether it should produce a book on the adaptation and extension of churches. The subject has become one of great importance both to the Church and to the conservation world. Some valuable contributions have been made to the debate. The Royal Fine Arts Commission inaugurated the discussion with its guidelines back in 1980 when, together with the then Historic Buildings Council, they announced that they were 'strongly opposed in principle to building in churchyards'. This advice was amplified in a further note of 1984. Among the dioceses, Chelmsford Diocesan Advisory Council (DAC) in 1990 launched a joint publication with Essex County Council called *So You Want to Extend Your Church?* which concentrated on the importance of producing acceptable designs and offered a variety of solutions. The Bishop's Council at Rochester issued a document the same year, *Reframing the Questions,* in which both re-ordering and new building were considered in more general terms. On the secular side, English Heritage published a well-illustrated appraisal of recent church extensions, although both illustrations and text found it easier to demonstrate what had gone wrong than what had gone right. Finally the Society for the Protection of Ancient Buildings issued a statement in 1991 outlining its philosophy as regards church extensions. It agreed with the Royal Fine Arts Commission that 'there should be a presumption against building in church-yards' but it also 'fully recognises that there is sometimes a need to provide new accommodation for the pastoral and social life of the church'.

So why should the Council for the Care of Churches add its voice when the various points of view seem already to have been expressed? We feel that there are four aspects of the question which have yet to be explored:

1

1. The process of designing church extensions or re-ordering schemes needs to be set out; first to lead parishes through the complex process of planning consent, both secular and ecclesiastical, and, second, to guide them towards solutions that are likely to prove acceptable and away from those that are not. The Council has unrivalled experience of buildings throughout the country from which to provide illustrations and evidence.

2. Parishes need assistance on the financial aspects of such schemes, especially fees and VAT. The Council is constantly involved in discussions with professional bodies and, through the ecumenical network of the Churches Main Committee, with national authorities.

3. The underlying pastoral and liturgical reasons for extensions and re-orderings have not been fully discussed. They need to be described and explained, not just asserted. As the only central Church body with a commitment to conservation, the Council should be the advocate to put the Church's case.

4. With its unique role at the centre, the Council can present a balanced view on Church art and buildings, drawing both on the experience of parishes and on the reactions of conservation bodies and amenity societies.

The four contributors to this booklet write from their own experience which represent different strands of the expertise of the Council. Two are priests, one a former archdeacon, now a bishop, with experience both of rural and urban areas; the other a liturgical expert who has known both parochial and cathedral ministry. Of the laymen, one is Secretary to a DAC, based in a diocesan office, who has for many years guided parishes through the technicalities of the process; the other is both a DAC Chairman and a practising conservation architect, working on ecclesiastical and secular buildings.

Each contribution is distinct, expressing its author's views on the particular subject. However, all share the Council's broad approach, which must comprehend an astonishing variety of circumstances. No church is the same as another, even if the design is similar; the furnishings, let alone the liturgical arrangements, will differ. It would be impossible as well as unwise to lay down one set of procedures as rules to be followed when considering alterations to a church. The following chapters are designed as signposts to point parishes towards what is right and practicable in their particular circumstances, not as barriers or hurdles to impede them.

Finally, before parishes even begin to plan layouts and elevations, we would urge them to consider the following points:

- The shape of the existing building and its relationship to its surroundings

- The real needs of the parish. Too often plans are set in motion through the enthusiasm of an individual or small groups or through a chance request and then are allowed to reach an advanced stage before simple questions of use and access are addressed.

They then should take themselves through the following list of questions:

1. Are there problem areas in and around the church which need improvement, e.g. former heating chambers either above or below ground, or unsightly or obsolete sheds housing a boiler or garden tools?

2. Is there a building in or near the churchyard which could be adapted for church use?

3. Is the church listed and if so, at what grade?

4. Has it received a grant from English Heritage or a similar body?

5. If a grant has been received, were conditions attached which might affect future work?

6. Is the church in a conservation area?

7. Are the trees in the churchyard listed?

8. Are there implications for the area contained in the development plans of the local authority?

9. Is the graveyard in use or has it been closed and placed in the care of the local authority? (See *The Responsible Care of Churchyards*, published by CCC in 1993)

10. Are the paths around the church rights of way?

11. What are the parking facilities at present and how would they be affected by any new proposals?

12. Are there any archaeological remains known to exist beneath the surface? Have there been previous surveys on the fabric, above or below ground?

13. If proposals involve plumbing and/or catering, is consideration being given to: i) health and safety factors, ii) the provision of drainage, iii) collection of rubbish.

14. Last but by no means least, has consideration been given to servicing and maintaining facilities in the future? Who will do the jobs and how easy will they be to perform quickly and efficiently? Plant, either existing or new, is only as good as the people who look after it.

Thomas Cocke has been secretary to the Council for the Care of Churches since 1990. He has served on the Listed Buildings Panels at Manchester and Cambridge, on the St Edmundsbury and Ipswich DAC and on committees of the Georgian Group and the Victorian Society.

1

Form and function: explaining the need

In this section I am writing about church extensions not from the viewpoint of a designer but as an archdeacon. For an archdeacon there are two priorities. One is to make connections between seemingly disparate objectives, mixing insights into prayer with considerations about drainage. Another is to distinguish between first-order and second-order concerns. The first-order task of the Church includes the call to worship, discipleship, mission and service. To achieve such first-order tasks, great attention needs to be given to such second-order tasks as parish boundaries, clergy stipends and the design of church extensions.

It has become something of a platitude that design form should follow function. In the case of a church, the Care of Churches Measure of 1991 has as its first clause the requirement that those concerned in our field 'should have due regard to the role of a church as a local centre of worship and mission'. To some degree local planners try to follow these terms of reference when considering adaptations or extensions to churches. However they tend to require each case to prove a statistical need about the numbers of people, or the number of meetings or the number of alternative meeting places. In most cases extensions are not being constructed simply to provide extra seating for worship: only one in twenty of recent cases in the Chelmsford Diocese came into this category. The issue is not so much about the amount of space as the use to which that space can be put.

'The case of need' has to be recognised as something more fundamental to the function of the church today. We must consider why so many parishes believe an extension is worth the effort of raising the money, and of facing all the negotiations with both church and secular authorities. There are major areas of change since the Victorian era, the last great period of church extensions. For example, the notion of 'Christendom' has become eroded, yet there has been a growing understanding of the congregation as the people of God. There are also different financial pressures. 'Plant' must be slimmed down, parish halls have moved from being relatively cheap but invaluable means of outreach, to being considered maintenance liabilities, and now capital assets.

The erosion of 'Christendom'

The first purpose of a church building is the worship of God through the ministry of word and sacrament. For centuries nurture in the Christian faith, which prompts that worship, has been woven into the fabric of our society. The young often began their Christian education at mother's knee. That learning continued in Church schools. So the church building served the function, reflected in its design, of being a place to which existing believers came for worship.

Now many people find their way to public worship seeking or hoping for faith, devoid of any Christian knowledge or experience. They may be responding to a variety of prompts: perhaps it has been effective pastoral care or powerful Christian witness. The church building can thus no longer be the place of worship alone but needs to be a place of nurture and training with spaces of the right shape and ambience.

It used to be that those worshipping together in the parish church already belonged by kinship and through their working lives to the same community. Now those who find themselves together for acts of worship may have no other connections with each other. So for worship to be real, a community needs to be created among those singing the same hymns, saying the same prayers and sharing the same Eucharist. Seeing no more of your neighbours in church than the backs of their heads was not a hindrance when you met each other constantly outside. Nowadays fellowship has to be created by sharing work or social events within the church. So, if design is to follow the function of fostering community among strangers, the wish for kitchen and lavatories becomes intelligible.

'The whole people of God'

There has been a recovery of the realisation that the Holy Spirit can be at work in the whole people of God. Congregations are changing from being passengers on a vessel captained by clergy to being fellow members of a crew. This increases the demand for learning and training. Different spaces are needed for different needs to be satisfied at the same time. For example, a basic provision might include at least a crèche for infants and rooms for children of different ages. For all ages the emphasis has changed from 'telling' to 'discovering', from 'explaining' to 'exploring'. The pulpit is no longer the major teaching base from which to communicate the Christian message to a congregation. People now learn together from one another in small groups, rather then in the single 'class-room' of the pewed church.

Liabilities into assets

After the Reformation different perceptions grew up of the right distinction between sacred and secular uses. By the nineteenth century the church building was set apart exclusively for formal worship, while the parish institutes and community halls were used for other, more secular activities such as games or drama. Now the local authority, private enterprise and voluntary groups have all become providers of varied community venues. Sometimes casual reference to church extensions for social purposes generates anxious resistance among those with both a sense that the sacred should be set apart and a memory that 'social' means barn dances and table tennis, if not worse. Unless the real reasons for a church extension are presented carefully in terms of nurture and community, people may fear that the church is betraying its task by secularising the very place which they believe it is charged to keep holy.

A congregation of sixty with both a church to seat 600 and a parish hall will be hard-pressed to keep both of them in good repair. Rationalisation can hardly be resisted. If the church building is used only for an odd hour each week, there may be little enthusiasm in the community to raise the money for maintenance, let along large-scale repair. In contrast, if an extension will develop the church building to accommodate contemporary needs, the congregation is more likely to grow, the will to give to be generated and the church building to be saved.

Many of those outside the Church still have to catch up with these changing needs and accept their implications for a church's function. There is a tendency for them to defend forms and designs which reflect the conditions of earlier days. For example, when the Royal Fine Art Commission stated its policy in 1980, it concluded, 'while appreciating the church's reasons for wanting additional accommodation, that it is strongly opposed in principle to building in churchyards.' Did they appreciate the true reasons? Fortunately they went on to recognise 'the need to look at each case on its own merits.'

There was less flexibility in the 1991 statement by the Society for the Protection of Ancient Buildings. 'The great majority of parish churches have grown or been altered over many centuries and have arrived at a state that makes it difficult to add to them without causing archaeological, historical or aesthetic damage.' It seems illogical that they can admit the first assertion and then suggest that this very process of growth and change should now cease.

The English Heritage guidelines are more encouraging. 'Most churches have been rearranged several times over the centuries to meet current liturgical needs and such changes are all part of the history of the building. English Heritage recognises that churches in active use must continue to adapt to the needs of our time. Our concern is to ensure that the historic fabric is respected and nothing of value irretrievably lost as a result of new work.'

Parochial Church Councils embarking on an extension need help in thinking through and then presenting their 'case of need' if they are to avoid resistance to their proposals at every level – from congregation, parishioners, amenity societies, local authorities and possibly English Heritage. The archdeacon, along with colleagues from the Diocesan Advisory Committee, can be powerful, informed advocates who accumulate and share experience from around the diocese or from further afield. They are well-placed to take initiatives such as guiding parishes to suitable designers or convening round table meetings to concentrate discussion and escape the cycle of accommodating the design to one party's wishes at the cost of alienating another's. If change is to happen creatively and extensions are to be built to the glory of God and as worthy enrichments of church life, then parishes need wise advice from the Church side, but also those outside the Church need advice and instruction on the real requirements of today's congregations.

Jonathan Bailey became Bishop of Derby in 1995. He was previously Vicar of Wetherby, Archdeacon of Southend and Bishop of Dunwich, and served on the Council for the Care of Churches 1990-92.

2

Space to celebrate: the liturgical aspects

Why undertake a liturgical reordering of the church building? The answer has to be to make the liturgy more effective. It must not be simply to conform to a fashion, or to make the church more adaptable, for instance for plays or concerts. The aim must be for the regular worship of the church to be offered in a setting likely to inspire devotion and to create the possibility of experiencing holiness.

The difficulty is that the liturgy does not simply take place in the building. At a certain level the building itself becomes part of the liturgy. Unless we worship with our eyes closed tight, part of what is offered will be the glass, the wood and stone, the shapes and curves and spaces, all mixed in with the prayer and the Scripture, the music and the silence. People are conscious of this when they go into a great cathedral, or a building of particular beauty, character or strong simplicity but tend to take it for granted as they worship week by week in the building with which they are most familiar. But it remains true, whether they are aware of it or not. It means that all liturgical reordering should be approached cautiously and hesitantly (even if the final design is bold and imaginative). Otherwise, in the apparent interest of good liturgy, something is created that is out of keeping with the glass and wood and stone, and even more so with the shapes and curves and spaces. Where the liturgical arrangement is fighting against the architecture, there will be a tension in the liturgy that will get in the way of true worship. The building can be modified, but in sympathy with the basic design, not against it.

The principal liturgical furnishings of the church are the altar, the pulpit/lectern and the font. Each of these will be considered in turn.

The **altar**, or holy table, is both a functional and a symbolic furnishing of the church. Its function is to provide the table for the celebration of the Eucharist. Its symbolism makes it a sacrament of the presence of Christ, which is an extension of its Eucharistic use. For the celebration of contemporary liturgy, the ideal is a free-standing altar in a generous, uncluttered space, behind which the ministers may stand facing the congregation, and round which the people may gather to receive the consecrated gifts.

This is not always achievable. Sometimes the creation of such an arrangement would mean the destruction of a fine altar and reredos. Sometimes there would not be sufficient space for the ministers to do more than squeeze between the table and the wall. Sometimes there would be nowhere suitable for the distribution of the sacrament. Sometimes a new altar would have to be erected too close to an existing one. In all these cases, the church needs to consider whether it might not be better to continue a more traditional arrangement with the celebration facing east. In any event, only the part of the service from the Offertory to the Distribution need be at the altar. Not only the whole Ministry of the Word but also the Post-Communion part of the rite can be celebrated elsewhere, for instance from a lectern at the chancel step.

The question of the relationship of one altar to another is important. Liturgically the ideal is one altar only in the main church (side chapels, separate rooms in effect, are a different matter). Two altars, acting as alternative foci of the presence of Christ, are confusing and unhelpful so, where possible, a reordering should move the altar, not add a second one. Where this is not possible, or would be aesthetically disastrous, care should be taken to ensure the primacy of the altar at which the Eucharist is normally to be celebrated. What is quite wrong is the addition of an insignificant free-standing table for the Eucharist, while an older larger altar

11

dominates behind. Also unsatisfactory is a scheme where, after a celebration at a nave altar, there is then a procession through the chancel to an older sanctuary for the distribution.

The shape and height of a free-standing altar need careful consideration. Altars against walls resemble sideboards, rectangular and tall. This is quite appropriate – sideboards look right against walls. But sideboards are not designed to be put in the middle of rooms. In the middle of a room a table is needed, perhaps a few inches lower then a 'sideboard' altar (though not too much if the celebration is to retain some dignity) and perhaps square or even round. Long rectangles for central altars are normally mistaken.

There are two other furnishings that need to be near the altar, though subsidiary to it: the credence table and the president's chair. The **credence table** provides a surface on which the vessels for the Eucharist are kept during the service, before and after they are required at the altar. The table is purely functional. It should draw as little attention to itself as possible but it should be sufficiently large to allow a satisfactory work surface, since a free-standing altar in full view of the people is not a proper setting for the ablutions that follow Communion.

More significant is the **president's chair**. People have often referred to the principal chair in the sanctuary as a 'Bishop's chair'. Technically of course there is no such thing except in a cathedral. It is that chair, the cathedra, which makes a church a cathedral church. Yet, a priest presiding at the liturgy does so as the bishop's deputy, and so it is not inappropriate that the chair used by the president at the Eucharist should be the chair in which the bishop sits when he comes and should carry his name.

This chair should be sufficiently different from other stools, chairs or benches in the sanctuary area that it clearly denotes its occupant as the president of the rite. It should not, however, be too grand and throne-like, like some Victorian sanctuary chairs. Its positioning is crucial. The occupant ought to have the whole assembly in view. The classic place for the chair is raised a little behind the table. Sometimes the chair may be to the side, but still facing the people, or angled towards them, providing the altar does not create a barrier between president and people. Reordering schemes that take no account of the place for the chair have missed an important aspect of a satisfactory liturgical arrangement.

The second major furnishing is the focus of the Word: reading the Scriptures and preaching. Traditionally in Anglican churches these two activities have each had a focus – **lectern** and **pulpit**. In some reorderings only one has been retained, with one focus for the Word, both read and preached. This focus, be it pulpit or lectern or, as Roman Catholics call it, 'ambo', needs to be of such a height that people can communicate from it, of such dignity that due honour is given to the place of the Word in the liturgy, and of a size and character that are in keeping with the altar. We hold Word and Sacrament in equal honour, and the focus of each in the church should reflect that. Altar and pulpit should not compete with but balance each other.

The third principal furnishing is the **font**. Like the lectern/pulpit it has an equal status to the altar. They are the foci of the two great sacraments of the Gospel, Baptism and Eucharist. In a reordering the font should not be made subsidiary to the altar, nor should it be given a portable or flimsy appearance where the altar seems solid and permanent. Ideally the font should have a space of its own, away from the altar focus and near the principal entrance, so that the people see it and pass by it whenever they come in to worship and also they can turn to it and see it in use when baptism is celebrated in the Sunday liturgy.

A number of factors militate against this in many churches. For instance, the principal entrance may be in a corner: space around the font may be cramped or pillars block the view. The solution too often is baptism out of a rose bowl set on a credence table at the chancel step, while the font remains neglected, a repository for flowers and leaflets. Here pastoral and liturgical principles sometimes have to compromise. One possibility is this: as with the Eucharist, it is possible to celebrate most of the baptismal liturgy away from the font, moving to it only for the part where water – and this should be more than a token drop – is crucial. Another is the repositioning of the font away from the door, perhaps near the altar. If this is to happen, the font must again have a significant space of its own.

Where a new font is to be designed, there are contemporary considerations that might lead to bold innovation. With the increase in adult baptism, a font should be designed to allow an adult at least to kneel in the water, yet to prevent more than one focus of baptism, it should also be suitable for the baptism of infants. Interesting new fonts are being made, of which one of the most splendid is that at Portsmouth Cathedral, that permit varieties of baptismal practice and should be studied in any reordering proposal. At the very least there should be the facility for sufficient water, possibly even flowing, and certainly visible. Rose bowls and ashtrays at the chancel step are not acceptable!

Two further considerations are also important in any reordering. One is the care that needs to be taken about the positioning of musicians, whether robed choirs or less formal singing groups, and of their instruments, whether organ or keyboards, flutes and guitars. The musicians are not performers who should dominate the liturgy but equally they are not separate from the congregation, to be banished to a gallery or transept where they do not feel part of the liturgical action. It is almost impossible to give specific guidance, for every church is different. However, in general the musicians need to be close to the liturgical action but not too close, and raised up but not too much.

Mention has been made of space. The altar, the lectern and the font all need their space. Very often the best reordering of a church involves simply the removal of excess furniture, without the addition of anything new. It is not just that the liturgy needs space for its movements, but that the space itself, unfilled by people or furniture, helps to create a sense of space in the soul, which is when true worship can begin to happen.

Michael Perham became Precentor at Norwich Cathedral in 1992. He was previously Team Rector of Oakdale in the Diocese of Salisbury. He was a member of the Council for the Care of Churches 1990-92 and has been a member of the Liturgical Commission since 1985.

3

Hoops and hurdles:
A guide to the consent process

It has to be said at the outset that obtaining the necessary consents, especially for works to the exterior, can be a complex and trying business. Much frustration will be avoided if at least one person involved with the project is thoroughly briefed about what consents will be required and how to obtain them.

Faculty Jurisdiction

Nearly all Church of England churches are subject to Faculty Jurisdiction, and nothing significant can be done to their fabric and furnishings without a licence, or 'faculty', which is granted by the Diocesan Chancellor. It follows that almost any scheme within the scope of this book will need a faculty. The Chancellor is guided, but not bound, by the advice of the Diocesan Advisory Committee (DAC). The primary job of the DAC is to consider any proposal from architectural, aesthetic, historical and technical points of view. It must either recommend a scheme to the Chancellor or report its reasons for being unable to do so.

The DAC does not ignore pastoral concerns. Under the Care of Churches Measure 1991, it must give 'due regard to the role of a church as a local centre of worship and mission'. However, in advising the Chancellor, its main concerns are related to the quality of the proposals before it, and it is for the Chancellor to decide whether pastoral or other concerns should override those of the DAC.

As PCC secretaries will know, there is a form to be completed known as a Petition for Faculty, to be accompanied by a PCC

Resolution. However these in themselves will not be sufficient to enable a DAC to discuss a scheme. The importance of proper illustrative plans and drawings cannot be over-emphasised. A full working specification will be required before the faculty can be granted and photographs, sketches and a copy of any design brief may also be helpful. DAC members require a lot of detail and spend much of their time trying to extract it from PCCs and their architects.

Preliminary advice from the DAC is there for the asking and an early site visit may well be of mutual benefit, before parishes become too committed to any particular proposal. This point has been made over and over again since the DAC system started some seventy-five years ago. Some parishes still seem unwilling to approach their DAC before submitting a cut-and-dried scheme, which it may be impossible to recommend for a number of reasons. It can save money as well as time and trouble to consult the DAC at an early stage, since the submission of the scheme which does not win DAC approval will have incurred costs for no benefit.

Most DACs meet monthly, but many take a summer break. They usually have a deadline some ten days before a meeting, after which they will not add a case to the agenda. Find out when the meeting deadlines are so as to minimise unnecessary delay. Make sure the DAC has all the information it needs, or time will be wasted. Ask the DAC secretary exactly what will be required at each stage. If a site visit is needed, ensure that you have available information to respond to members' points but do not expect answers on the spot. DACs will only give their formal advice after an opportunity for full discussion at the next DAC meeting.

What happens if a DAC cannot approve a scheme, or if someone else, such as a group of parishioners, objects to the PCC's proposal? The answer is that a Consistory Court hearing may be required, at which the Chancellor will hear all the arguments and will make a decision. Usually such a hearing will take place at the church itself.

On the whole, it is best if a disputed matter can be settled by correspondence or site meeting, but it may be that there is no alternative to a formal hearing.

English Heritage: subsequent works clause

Has your church ever received grant-aid from English Heritage (EH)? If so, any significant alteration to the building requires their written consent. This may take a little while to obtain but Chancellors will not grant a faculty until any necessary consent is submitted. Any work carried out without this consent jeopardises future generations' chances of obtaining further EH grant-aid.

Write to English Heritage, either to the inspector for the region or the commissioned architect. She/he will need at least as much information as the DAC and may well need to visit the church before making a judgement, so allow time for this part of the process. A joint EH/DAC/PCC site meeting at an early stage could save time and avoid frustration. The need for early consultation cannot be overstressed.

EH will not be unreasonable in considering schemes for adaptation. Like DACs they have to be conscious of the needs of the worshipping community. On the other hand, they are acting to safeguard the historical and artistic qualities of the buildings on which public money has already been spent and for which more could be requested in the future. It is also fair to say that the cautious approach of EH has sometimes been of positive value in refining schemes or in deflecting over-hasty short-term solutions.

Archaeology

A sizeable proportion of church adaptation work will involve archaeology, and remember this means work on the standing fabric as well as holes in the ground. Typically alterations involving drainage or heating appliances or changes to and at floor level may call for archaeological observation and recording. The cost of archaeological work needs to be included in the budget from the outset. Your DAC archaeological consultant should be asked at an early stage whether archaeology is likely to be an important issue. A relatively modern church may stand on a site of much interest which could be destroyed by careless excavation.

Building regulations

Certain categories of building works, including some which are purely internal, will involve the need for building regulations approval. These include anything involving drainage. This is usually straightforward, and is best dealt with by your architect. Fees are always chargeable by the local authority, both for determining the application and inspecting work in progress.

External works

If the consents discussed so far sound rather complex, there is more to come if extension or new building are involved. In these cases it is even more essential that the architect and the PCC know what is required, and that they adopt a step-by-step strategy.

Any new building or demolition, or other work which materially affects the appearance of a church, will require planning consent under the Town and Country Planning Act 1990, which also involves an application fee. Churches are not exempt from planning control, as is sometimes mistakenly thought.

However the great many churches listed by the Department of National Heritage as buildings of architectural or historic importance (Grades I, II* or II) are exempt from the need to obtain listed building consent for most categories of alteration or demolition work if they are churches in use. This 'Ecclesiastical Exemption' from the effects of historic building law is something which the Church of England enjoys by virtue of the proven operation of its own parallel planning system, the Faculty Jurisdiction.

If an application is made for planning permission to extend or alter the appearance of a listed church, or to build something next to it, the planning authority will naturally be guided by the listed status of the church, and may consult with EH or with the recognised amenity societies, such as the Society for the Protection of Ancient Buildings, the Georgian Group or the Victorian Society. If a church is listed I or II* (or II within Greater London) the planning authority must consult with EH and take account of its comments.

Where planning permission is needed it would be advisable to make a preliminary approach to the planning authority at an early stage. There may be important aspects such as parking, visibility, highway access, etc, which may have a far-reaching effect on overall feasibility.

Churchyards

Many schemes for extension or new building work will involve the churchyard. This introduces added complications, but not to the extent that people sometimes think. The legal provisions affecting churchyards are set out usefully in the *Churchyards Handbook* (published for the Council for the Care of Churches by Church House Publishing 1988) and *Responsible Care for Churchyards* (published for the Council for the Care of Churches by Church House Publishing 1993). Each case is different and you should consult the Diocesan Registrar at the outset, particularly if there is likely to be disturbance to burials or memorials.

The extension of a church into its churchyard can be done by faculty. Full details of any graves affected will be required, and the Chancellor may direct special efforts to be made to trace relatives of anyone buried in the area which is to be disturbed. Regard must also be given to the Disused Burials Ground Act of 1884 which forbade building in churchyards, except to extend the church – a concept which is now of wider interpretation than it was in the 1880s.

An alternative approach is via the Pastoral Measure 1983, where Section 30 provides for redundancy of all or part of a churchyard. This removes the legal effects of consecration and may be felt appropriate for such a project as a church hall, where much of the use of the facility may be secular in nature. The land which thus becomes redundant will cease to be benefice property and will normally be vested in the Board of Finance, to be held on behalf of the PCC. If the Pastoral Measure approach is to be followed, the PCC should contact the secretary of the Diocesan Pastoral Committee to discuss the procedure and mechanics of what is required. The process involves extensive consultation under the Pastoral Measure, and will take a minimum of nine months to achieve.

Jonathan MacKechnie-Jarvis has been secretary to the Gloucester DAC since 1986. He has served as treasurer to his PCC and as a Council member of the Gloucester Historic Churches Trust.

4

Money matters: financial planning

How is the work to be paid for? In some instances, the PCC will have the benefit of some cash windfall – for example from the sale of an inconvenient hall somewhere. In such cases the usual problems of fund raising may not apply, but even so thought must be given to various aspects of financial control. To be dependent on a private donor, however generous, may also create problems for the control and management of the project.

At the other end of the spectrum is the case where the bulk of the cost must be raised from scratch, and the viability of the project is dependent on the success of an appeal.

Control

The methods of financial control will obviously vary according to the nature and scale of the project, but in all cases they must be accorded a proper attention from the outset. Many parish projects have run into difficulties because of a lack of financial foresight and realism.

Who will be in charge of the project finances? The PCC treasurer may feel that he or she has enough to do already and that someone else needs to be found to do the extra work. Co-ordination of effort and control could then become an issue.

The Diocesan Stewardship Department may be able to help with advice about sources of finance, covenanting and Gift-Aid. If a centralised covenant scheme is in operation, the PCC should consider participating. In a major appeal, professional assistance with fund raising may be a possible option, but the level of fees could prove prohibitive.

Accurate financial targets are needed from the earliest possible stage. It is fundamental that budgeted costs should be realistic and should include margins for contingencies and over-spend. There is a human tendency for serious over-optimism in the early stages of a project, which is ample justification for constant questioning by the treasurer as to whether everything foreseeable has been taken into account.

VAT

A much-needed church extension in the South West Midlands ran into financial trouble for two reasons, both of which could and should have been readily apparent at the outset. These were VAT and stage payments. With VAT currently at 17.5%, the former aspect is now of key importance.

In the case under consideration, no account had been taken of VAT because it was understood that the work would be zero-rated. Unfortunately this belief was based on incomplete advice, and the true position was only clarified with HM Customs and Excise after the decision to go ahead had been taken. The position on VAT for extensions has changed since that instance took place.

In all cases the VAT status of the project ought to be established at the outset, both as to building work, fitting out and professional fees. If any doubt exists, write to the local Customs and Excise office, setting out your case, and then be prepared to negotiate.

Stage payments

The other serious financial problem in the case mentioned above related to the timing of payments. Architect and contractors alike will in most large projects require stage payments as the work progresses. The financial plan must therefore take into account timing of cash demands and availability of ready funds. It is not sufficient that the overall cash requirement should more or less balance anticipated income, if cash deficiencies may arise during the contract period.

In order to avoid difficulty, the project treasurer should find out in detail how and when the architect (and any other professional adviser such as the structural engineer or quantity surveyor) will charge and calculate fees and expenses, and at what point interim accounts will be due. VAT is always payable on fees and needs to be taken into consideration. Similarly, contractors' proposals for stage payments need to be as clear as possible.

It need hardly be said that even an abortive project may incur considerable professional fees. Many church architects carry out a great deal of preparatory drawing work for schemes which never get off the ground, and PCCs are often astonished to be presented with fee accounts!

Sources of funds

So far we have been largely discussing outflow of funds. A word must now be said about the various sources of finance available for church projects. Mention has already been made of the one-off cash windfall situation e.g. sale of property or perhaps a substantial legacy. Beyond this, the main sources are:

- Giving from within the parish
- Grants from other organisations
- Loans

Giving

There are clearly various ways in which local giving may be stimulated and organised. Parish experience seems to show that people will respond to targets for a tangible project. Indeed, a properly organised appeal may bring together the congregation and the wider parish community into a joint effort, and even provide a platform for evangelism.

An appeal is usually best co-ordinated by a small group under a dynamic and efficient leader, preferably with some experience of fund-raising. A professional attitude of mind is needed. The PCC may have to advance money for printing of stationery and other expenses.

The main task of such an appeals committee will be to stimulate fund-raising efforts and to avoid a clash of activities or – a common problem – well-meant events which involve a great deal of effort but which are likely to raise only a small amount after expenses are paid.

The project treasurer should be fully aware of the advantages of Gift-Aid. As amended in 1994, this scheme allows very simple recovery of income tax for one-off payments of £250 or more. The Diocesan Stewardship Department should be able to give useful advice on this scheme, which is of the greatest importance in dealing with one-off gifts.

For gifts under £250 the older Deposited Covenant Scheme is still available, but the paperwork is a little more complex. Conventional four year covenants for successive planned gifts should also be used as far as possible, and may be of great value in encouraging longer-term support such as for the repayment of loans.

Grants

An approach will naturally be made to appropriate grant-making trusts. There are a number of organisations which are dedicated to the repair and conservation of church fabric, but these are unlikely to be of assistance for extension or adaptation work. On the other hand the Diocesan Board of Finance may well operate a scheme for grant-aiding parish development projects, as well as straight repairs.

The most useful source of information will be the *Directory of Grant-Making Trusts* which is published by the Charities Aid Foundation. This is available at most public libraries and contains a wealth of information about the trusts which are listed, including their relative wealth and areas of special interest.

The Directory contains some salutary advice on how to present an application. Appeal committees are urged to read and re-read the sections concerned. Parishes should be ready for quite a high proportion of disappointing replies, but it pays to be persistent. Not surprisingly, many grant-giving bodies are inundated with appeals for help, and it is important to be well organised, clear and enthusiastic. A personal approach is of great benefit: apart from making use of any pre-existing connections or contacts, a telephone call to follow up a written request for help may well be of benefit and may make your appeal stand out from others.

Building projects in Urban Priority Areas (UPAs) may be eligible for help from the Church Urban Fund. In most cases it will be necessary for the scheme to be part of some type of community project, and all applications must be approved and submitted by the diocesan bishop. In such cases there may also be the possibility of grants from local authorities or from central government sources, especially if there is an element of job creation, as well as a benefit to the wider community.

In all cases, consideration should be given to an appeal to business organisations in the local area. The main reference library will be able to provide lists of local firms. A letter to the company secretary should set out the needs and resources of the appeal as well as emphasising the benefits of the project and the efforts which are being made to raise funds locally. Note that the Gift-Aid Scheme is applicable to companies in much the same way as it is to individual tax payers.

Loan finance

It may be worth taking out loans to enable the work to proceed in one continuous operation whilst fund-raising is going on, and to assist cash flow wherever money available is tied up in deposit accounts. Obviously this will be dependent on the ability of the parish to cope with the burden of repayment. If the project work has been paid for partly by means of a loan, some of the impetus for fund-raising will have been lost and it may not be easy to encourage support to pay off the loan – a situation worsened by any interest which may be payable.

It may be possible to find loan finance on favourable terms (perhaps even interest-free) from members of the congregation. Alternatively the Diocesan Board of Finance may operate a loan scheme. The Incorporated Church Building Society may be able to offer an interest-free loan for certain categories of extension work. Other possibilities include the Central Board of Finance and the Ecclesiastical Insurance Group, both of whom may make loans in appropriate circumstances.

Summary

The above notes are not of course in any way exhaustive, but may be useful in summarising the main areas concerned.

An imaginative and vigorous approach, coupled with realism and commonsense, is as important to the financial health of the project as it is to the architectural aspect.

The project treasurer should be ready to make use of all the help that is available, both in tax benefits (e.g. Gift-Aid) and in seeking out possible areas of outside funding.

Jonathan MacKechnie-Jarvis has been secretary to the Gloucester DAC since 1986. He has served as treasurer to his PCC and as a Council member of the Gloucester Historic Churches Trust.

5

Practical problems and possibilities: the design aspects

This section discusses the practical problems and opportunities that may occur when undertaking schemes for alteration or extension to parish churches. As mentioned above, recent publications on the subject have tended to be negative in their recommendations and in their lack of confidence in the capacity of contemporary designers to conceive of solutions that do honour to the quality and character of our parish churches. These views are generally taken from one perspective – that of care and conservation of the historic fabric and its contents.

The ecclesiastical system of control, however, charges those having the care of our churches with a wider responsibility. Care and conservation remain their primary duty but decisions must be taken in the wider context, keeping the parish church alive and in use as a local centre of worship and mission. This continuity of use is critical to the survival of the buildings themselves, as is acknowledged within the secular legislation and guidance (e.g. in the Government's PPG 15 and in English Heritage's *New Work in Historic Churches*). Some concessions to continued use are therefore justified in the interests of preserving the whole. This difficult balancing act of permitting change without compromising the character of the historic structure is at the centre of the ecclesiastical control system. Whatever its faults, this system has maintained our historic churches in as good a state of repair as might have been expected had they been under the secular system (as revealed in the English Heritage analysis, *Buildings at Risk*).

In reviewing church alterations over the last thirty years, it is difficult not to conclude that they have often, despite the safeguards built into the system, detracted from the quality of the original buildings. As with a great deal of the secular architecture of the period, much of the work carried out so vigorously in the 1950s and 60s now looks dated and rather embarrassing. There seem fewer successes than failures.

However they serve as lessons of the importance in alteration and extension work of the following issues:

Siting

Untold damage can be done by choosing the wrong spot in which to place new work. There must always be a preference for siting new work discreetly. Particularly on extensions, a bold scheme in a concealed area will often fit in without visual damage, whereas a modest piece of work in a prominent position will have an unacceptable impact. The archaeological implications also need to be considered.

Scale

The relationship of size and massing of the new work is all important. The new should generally be subservient to the old and avoid being intrusive or dominant. However there needs to be a proper balance; too domestic a scale in new work can make it appear inadequate by comparison with the existing building.

Form and detail

Much visual judgement depends on the perception of relationships between different elements within a composition and between the work of art and its setting. The eye will accept more comfortably shapes and forms that seem in context or are present in the existing building. This is not to argue for direct pastiche, but rather that the sources for the new design should be sought in the old. Reinterpretation of traditional themes can give ample opportunity for originality and pleasure, with the new work unashamed in declaring its age. Lethaby, writing in 1924, declared that new work should, in the context of historic buildings, be 'as unobtrusive as possible and frankly modern'. For the same reason, English Heritage urge that details of new work should not be given a spurious ecclesiastical pedigree.

Materials

Some of the most successful schemes rely for their effect on the use of traditional high quality materials and restrained detail. On extensions, simple forms in natural well-laid stone with a pitched roof of tile or slate can produce a dignified and harmonious scheme.

Quality of design

The published guides to church alteration urge that new design should be played down so as not to challenge but rather to act as a foil to the existing building (see above). This emphasis on subordination in scale and style has often been taken to the point of plain dullness. An anxiety to be self-effacing at all costs can lead to a design being so insipid that it diminishes the existing building.

For a design to be successful it needs not only to satisfy its function but to contain an added quality of visual stimulus and pleasure – what Sir Henry Wootton in the seventeenth century called 'Delight'. These elements can be stated unobtrusively. It is, however, noticeable that successful church alterations – be they kitchen cupboards, aisle screens or large extensions – are those where the designers have the creative skill and confidence to inform their work with something positive and pleasurable. This underlines the importance of choosing the right designer for the right job.

Getting ready

Many of the schemes referred to below are modest, deliberately intended to show examples more typical of the everyday problems encountered in a parish church, than might be achieved by illustrating grander but less relevant schemes. As has often been observed, there can be no rigid rules to direct parishes in undertaking schemes of alteration. Within certain basic considerations, success results from attitude and skill, not from following a formula. No two churches are the same and so the best solution must vary according to the individual circumstances.

The two key elements in preparing successful schemes of alteration, are the definition of a precise brief of what is required, and the selection of a suitable designer for the project. These two elements are closely related. The brief cannot and should not be fully settled without the involvement of the designer. It should be the designer who provides practical answers to the problems and demands posed by the requirements given in the brief.

Defining the brief

Defining the brief is no easy matter. The Royal Fine Arts Commission has suggested that most schemes for alteration to churches have little to do with essential needs and everything to do with convenience. This remark shows a misunderstanding of the changing role of the parish church over the last half-century. As chapter 1 demonstrates, the parish church is now expected to act as the community centre for Christian activity and worship throughout the parish. This sets new demands on buildings, which have already absorbed the effects of similarly dramatic changes in worship and social patterns over the centuries. Nonetheless it is of the utmost importance in refining the brief to scrutinise and exclude anything that is not essential. Ideas can often spring from enthusiasm, from a desire to demonstrate an outwards and visible sign of Christian vitality, rather than from a carefully considered

31

and tested long-term need. Inevitably some compromise will be called for where a degree of convenience will have to be sacrificed to maintain the balance between use and conservation. Occasionally the character and architectural quality of a church are so much of a piece that no amount of skilful compromise is possible, but such cases are rare.

Choosing the right designers

The critical importance of choosing the right designers has already been stressed. They will have the perception to see the new work in context with the history on display and as its natural successor within the church. Sensitivity and empathy with the building are essential, not only for the visual and functional success of the scheme, but for its safe passage through the complex legislative controls. The creative qualities required in even the simplest work of alteration mean that someone with the proper design abilities and training is called for. In practice this would require an architect, although on furniture and fittings it may be equally appropriate to involve a craftsman designer, possibly working with the architect.

The selection of a suitable designer is usually a matter of thorough research and careful judgement by the parish. Good design skills, even exceptional design skills, need cost no more than the utilitarian. One obvious choice would be the architect retained by the parish to carry out the quinquennial inspections. Such a person will know both the structure, and the parish's needs and expectations. However there may be cases when the inspecting architect feels too close to the building as it is to find it easy to stand back and take a fresh look at a new problem. Other architects may recognise that their speciality lies in repair rather than in new work, and that it would be more appropriate to employ someone else to deal with the project. Matters such as liturgical reordering are highly specialised. The parish should be prepared to discuss the matter openly and frankly with the inspecting architect before reaching a decision.

Vetting architects

Richard Carr-Archer, writing in the 1992 issue of *Churchscape* on the subject of 'Choosing an Architect', stated that 'Architects come in all shapes and sizes, like suits of clothes, and are capable of all sorts of use. But few garments can be used for all purposes – all the time – and so it is with architects'. He then went on to discuss the specialised skills required to meet the demands of new work to churches, acknowledging the potential role of the craftsman-designer. He concluded that if the parish is contemplating major alterations, the selection process should include: checking for advice on names with the local and adjacent DACs, talking to other parishes who have undertaken similar projects and inspecting the results, asking the architects/designers under consideration to submit details and illustrations of their work, preparing any interviews with care. The parish should not be in a rush to make a selection. The practice of inviting sketch ideas from short-listed architects is not to be recommended, as it misses out the proper evolutionary process of the design brief through consultation. It can lead to the parish not only selecting an idea rather than a designer but also becoming attached to a scheme that might, with more mature consideration, have been shown as inappropriate.

When to involve the architect

It is false economy for a parish to delay the involvement of their selected architect. An architect's skills are important at an early stage, in analysing and balancing the elements of the initial brief presented to them by their clients, in drawing out other relevant considerations and in sifting the assembled information to extract the most crucial problems to be solved. This process also permits the designer's vision and creative originality to mesh with the functional requirements of the brief. A careful start takes time, but protects the parish from spending money unwisely and from unnecessary meddling. No amount of professional skill later can disguise a project that is essentially flawed in its conception.

As professionals, architects expect to be paid for their advice and skills. However, many will be generous with their time in giving advice to a parish in the early stages of a scheme and will understand a parish's predicament. It is essential that the parish should establish with their advisers the precise extent of their financial commitment for professional fees before instructing any work.

Budget and fees

A vital part of any brief is the budget available. Finance is discussed in greater detail in chapter 4 but the budget given to the architect/designer must be realistic for the brief: it must be small enough to be managed by the parish, and generous enough for the intended work to be carried out to a standard appropriate to its setting. If structural work is involved or foundations are a problem, it is likely that a structural engineer will need to be employed by the parish at the appropriate stage. Even on smaller projects, the involvement of a quantity surveyor can make sense. As specialist cost consultants, they can enable a much tighter control to be kept on expenditure and ensure that the projected costs are within the budget set. On a large scheme, the appointment of mechanical and electrical consultants may also be worthwhile.

In the early stages, long before work begins on site, the parish will need to budget for the proportion of fees due to the architect, a structural engineer and quantity surveyor (if required), for legal and administrative charges by the Diocese and local authority, and for the relevant VAT. No building work can be instructed until the parish has the funds readily available to meet the financial terms of the building contract. Failure to pay on time can break a contract, so reliance must not be placed on uncertain promises of assistance or of grant to meet the required cash flow. The parish should also look beyond the completion of the project. Can they continue to maintain and run both existing and new buildings, even after their finances are depleted by the cost of the project?

Study what is there

As mentioned above, a careful study of the building as it stands and of its historical evolution will help in finding the best solution for any alterations. Respect and understanding for what is there – the need, as Alexander Pope put it, to 'consult the genius of the place in all' – ensure that new work follows the grain of the building and is thus integrated with it. Even a cursory glance at the average parish church will reveal a sequence of significant changes over the centuries. The elasticity of the Vicar of Bray's beliefs has been paralleled by the adaptability of our medieval churches. There is nothing new about churches being altered to accommodate the changing liturgy and enthusiasms of successive generations. The cumulative effects of these changes are significant parts of the interest and pleasure of churches. The closer any new proposals can be brought to the established pattern of form and growth in an individual building, the greater the chance of the new work proving successful. The parish's research and preparation should be extended to include the archaeology and ecology of the church and churchyard, so that the full impact of any proposals can be properly assessed. The DAC will be able to give guidance on these aspects.

Existing buildings may be scattered

Many churches are provided with separate church halls, parish offices and, though this is less common today, parsonages large enough to house parish functions. These buildings may be close to the church but sited outside the churchyard, or may have been deliberately placed at some distance to spread the church's physical presence within a larger parish.

Consideration of providing new facilities off-site

Alterations to churches are rarely required to accommodate an increased congregation. More often the required facilities are of a social and community nature. It may therefore make more sense to leave the existing church unaltered and to provide what is needed, either as part of the parish's buildings elsewhere or as a new development away from the church. Where the church and churchyard do not lend themselves to alteration this can provide the answer. It is usually the most sympathetic on conservation grounds. The green open spaces which surround the majority of our churches are as priceless an asset as the church fabric itself.

The case for and against erecting a separate building

English Heritage prefer any new accommodation to be provided in a separate building in order to minimise the impact on the historic building and its setting. This view conflicts with that of the Royal Fine Arts Commission, which considers that any new structures within the churchyard are almost inevitably detrimental to this special quality of English parish churches, and that even a building placed on the extremity of the churchyard is a second-best solution.

An additional complication is that building in a churchyard closed to burial is forbidden under the Disused Burial Grounds Act 1884, unless the building is attached to the church and can count as an extension to it. This obstacle can be overcome by declaring part of the churchyard redundant, through a Pastoral Scheme (see page 21). A problem common to any new construction work in the graveyard, be it for a separate building or an extension, is that provision needs to be made for the resiting of monuments and the reinterment of any human remains disturbed by the work. This will involve a lengthy and complicated legal process and also considerable tact to avoid giving offence to surviving relatives. New foundations can be designed in such a way as to minimise disturbance to earlier burials.

Two fairly typical examples of new detached building projects were those for All Saints, Oakham, Rutland (1991) and for St Michael, Budbrooke, Warwickshire (1992). In neither case was the outcome fully satisfactory, in part due to the complexity of the secular and ecclesiastical control systems. At Oakham, the parish proposed, after consultation with English Heritage, to put up a new parish room, classroom, lavatories and kitchen block to the north of the fine fourteenth-century church, the quality of which, both inside and outside, is such as to make internal subdivision unacceptable. The design brief agreed with English Heritage was for a 'modest unobtrusive functional building' with no physical link to the church. The resultant proposals satisfied this brief exactly, but no one else. The proposed building seemed to lack character yet its bulk would have been an intrusion, interrupting the flow of open space around the church. Despite the parish's efforts, the scheme was refused Listed Building Consent and was abandoned. At Budbrooke, similar consultations took place and the architect's original conception was modified and simplified at the direction of the planning authorities to bring its form closer to that of a vernacular brick barn. The new building is sited on the extreme edge of the churchyard. The facilities inside are admirable for a growing parish, but the size and unbroken external form are in danger of dominating the church itself.

Internal adaptation

The majority of church alteration work in the last thirty years has involved adaptation of the existing structure, rather than new extension. Extensions are disruptive and expensive solutions, which should only be adopted when they are the only way of meeting the parish's needs. Internal adaptations, even of modest scale and impact, can often achieve the same objectives. Small adjustments can produce significant advantages in worship or in the flexibility of use of the building.

Adaptations should, as indicated above, show a proper respect for the historic structure, avoiding damage to the original and should be, if practicable, removable. Fashions and needs change and alterations made now may well need to be undone by a future generation. The position, scale, form, materials and design must be carefully considered in this context.

The most common requirements for alteration to parish churches are for improved social and 'comfort' facilities. As has been emphasised in this booklet, the parish church is now expected to perform a much wider communal role than hitherto. If it fails to fulfil this role satisfactorily, if it fails to act effectively as a 'local centre of worship and mission' in all its facets, it may threaten the spiritual growth of the parish. The church building must work as a meeting place, in which people can gather conveniently and happily together. The social dynamics of meeting, as well as the requirements of the liturgy, will play a significant part in any reordering. This should not be taken as an invitation to fill our churches with fitted carpets and armchairs. Even well-intentioned desire for increased comfort and convenience can be destructive of a church's internal character.

There is a correlation between the intensity of use and the spiritual vitality of a parish. However some compromise can be tolerated in the interests of preserving the historic fabric. It may be better, as William Morris stressed, to suffer some little inconvenience now in the interests of preserving something irreplaceable and precious for posterity.

Where an interior is all of a piece, fitted out at a single period, surviving intact and of significant quality, adaptation or reordering may sometimes be impossible without unacceptable damage to the predominant architectural character. This applies as much to a vivid polychromatic nineteenth-century interior such as St Mary, Studley Royal, Yorkshire, as to a finely furnished eighteenth-century design such as St Mary Magdalene, Stapleford, Leicestershire. In such cases the parish may have to accept the position as it is, and seek other ways of satisfying their requirements. There have been exceptional cases where the extent of acceptable alteration needs to be balanced against the survival of the building. This dilemma can only be resolved by a consistory court. The Victorian Society considered that at St Jude, Southsea the interior would be totally changed by the proposed alterations, but others argued that this solution offered the only prospect for the repair and survival of the exterior which makes a significant contribution to the townscape.

Typical needs

DACs receive frequent applications from parishes for providing lavatory or coffee-making and drinking facilities. Next in order of popularity must come the creation of small meeting rooms for use by a sunday school or children's group, and by a crèche during the Family Communion services. Larger parish rooms or meeting spaces are often required if there is no parish hall nearby. A decision may be made to site the parish office within the church to give a more permanent presence in the building, both to welcome visitors and to act as a deterrent to vandals. Not unreasonably the clergy or choir may feel that the traditional broom-cupboard-sized vestries are inadequate for their needs in robing or preparation. It can be encouraging to bell ringers to provide more convenient and accessible ringing chambers, whether at the base of a tower or higher up. Sometimes better arrangements are needed for permanent storage in the church, particularly if furniture is moved around to suit differing uses. Provision for the disabled must be considered. The parish and its incumbent will be giving constant thought to ways of improving worship or making the building seem more welcoming to visitors. This can, as discussed above, be achieved by careful reordering of the interior. A successful reordering can enliven worship and give new meaning and relevance to the architectural qualities of the church. Urban churches, particularly those in more run-down areas, can have special needs which may involve the introduction of related community or even commercial uses.

Schemes of adaptation

It is rare nowadays for internal alterations to be required to accommodate a growing congregation. However such schemes have been carried out, usually by the provision of west galleries within the nave. Care needs to be taken to ensure satisfactory sight-lines and acoustics for those in the gallery.

Schemes for the provision of coffee-making facilities should involve minimal disturbance to the interior. English Heritage's booklet, *New Work in Churches,* illustrates the kitchen area at St Michael, Thorpe-le-Soken, Essex which is housed within a simple and dignified tall range of cupboards set against the aisle wall (see illustration below). As well as removing the visual clutter normally associated with crockery and sinks, these cupboards are sufficiently assured in the elegance and restraint of their design and the excellence of their materials to sit quite happily within the church. An even more discreet scheme is that at St Lawrence, Mickleton, Gloucestershire (1990), where the whole kitchen is contrived within a double-doored cupboard tucked into the space below the old west organ gallery. What tends to get overlooked in assessing the impact of

St Michael, Thorpe-le-Soken, Chelmsford Diocese: cupboard at W end of S aisle enclosing kitchen facilities.

such schemes is, on the one hand proper ventilation, and on the other plumbing and drainage, which often involve the laying of new drains or water services across the churchyard. The resultant excavations and disturbance of the outer fabric of the church can present archaeological problems and should be carefully considered in advance. In some churches the water is carried in and the sink waste run into a removable bucket but this is only a makeshift solution.

Vestry areas often lend themselves well to adaptation provided they are of sufficient size. At St Gregory, Tredington, Warwickshire (1987) the nineteenth-century vestry was fitted out with lavatory, lobby, sink and new cupboards for robes; a stair was inserted leading to a gallery to make a small office area for the incumbent, all within the original space. This portmanteau scheme proved slightly too condensed in use but perhaps makes the point that congregations should aim to fit as much as possible into the smallest possible space. By keeping spaces usable but compact a surprising amount can be fitted in and the effects of change contained. Even more modest in its impact was the conversion of the space behind the organ in St Benet, Cambridge (1989) to form, together with a small addition beyond, a simple kitchen and lavatory facility (see illustration overleaf) .

Another popular way of creating greater flexibility within the church is by a partial removal of pews. Such a solution cannot be countenanced where the pews themselves are an essential part of the church's internal architectural scheme: the partial removal, for instance, of pews from a fully box-pewed church can radically compromise and change the integrity of an historic interior. However the majority of churches have inherited a mixed legacy of pews of varying visual or historic interest. It often makes sense to clear modern pews to create an open area, although this will usually also involve the lowering of the raised timber floors left behind. At Holy Trinity, Stroud (1991) a meeting space on a grand scale has been formed by font resiting and pew removal. In this case the new space lies below the west gallery and

St Benet, Cambridge, Ely Diocese: modest kitchen/lavatory extension at E end of the N aisle.

the sense of openness contrasts tellingly against the clutter of the earlier layout. The removal and resetting of original features, where these are to be resited as part of a scheme of adaptation, must be treated with great care if they are to preserve their architectural coherence. A set of early nineteenth-century box pews surviving at the west end of the nave at St James, Hanslope, Buckinghamshire is to be adapted to fit at the west end of the south aisle in a way that keeps them largely intact and makes them usable within the parish's intended flexibility for the rest of the church.

The removal of chancel screens is sometimes proposed in order to open up the sanctuary to the congregation. Screens may on occasion be a visual impediment but they can also give a separate identity to a space. Their removal can detract from any sense of mystery and holiness within the sanctuary, without significant benefits in other ways.

Removal and resiting of fittings within the church are often part of a general liturgical reordering. Any change to the internal layout needs to be considered in the context of the whole and of the future needs and intentions of the parish. A pioneering reordering at St Peter and St Paul, Northleach, Gloucestershire (1961) skilfully inserted, behind the new nave altar, an open wrought-iron screen of sufficient visual weight to check the eye and to define the separate chapel in the chancel beyond. The displaced choir were boldly placed, along with the resited organ, to provide a musical focus in the north aisle.

Recent reorderings of particular sensitivity and skill at Birmingham, Portsmouth and Hereford Cathedrals serve as examples of how such changes can draw unexpected qualities from an existing building and bring new meaning to worship. Although examples set by cathedrals should not automatically be seen as appropriate precedents for alteration to parish churches – something that may make sense in a grand setting can prove inappropriate in more modest surroundings – it is often to cathedrals and their architects that parish churches can look for enlightened and imaginative ideas.

Subdividing a church

Any subdivision within a church needs to be carefully handled in order to preserve the volumes and flow of space that were integral to the architectural quality of the original. Glazed screens are often proposed for this reason, but glass has to be set within a frame and the substance of this, combined with reflections on the glass, can create a significant visual barrier. Screens, whether solid or transparent, should therefore be set in positions that make sense within the architectural scheme of the church. Like screens of earlier ages, they should have the benefit of being easily moved later. At St Peter, Stoke Lyne, Oxfordshire (1992), where it was proposed to divide off the nave for social purposes, the Council for the Care of Churches considered it was important for the screen to be aligned on a roof truss so the division did not appear arbitrary.

It may sometimes be sensible to block off the chancel completely, reducing the congregational space and providing a separate and usable space within the old chancel. This has been done successfully at St Nicholas, Warwick (1989), where the chancel was a later addition, not wholly in sympathy with the eighteenth-century church (illustrated opposite). The chancel arch is blocked by slightly recessed walls to create a parish room in the chancel behind.

Side aisles or transepts will often lend themselves to subdivision. At St Michael, Thorpe-le-Soken, Essex, a meeting room was created by screening off the western end of the south aisle with carefully proportioned sheets of glass, set in a simply detailed, unfussy but dignified oak frame. It is a good example of the English Heritage recommendation that, where screens are set on the line of arcades, they should be put behind the columns to allow the full mouldings of the earlier architectural features still to be read.

A similar scheme, but using bronze-anodised metal for the glazed screens, has been formed in the south west corner of St Matthew, Salford Priors, Warwickshire (1992), where the design is more boldly stated but is still not distracting visually from the historic fabric (see illustration on page vi). With the minimum of disturbance the parish have achieved a small meeting room and a kitchen, ingeniously contrived below the west window of the room behind a plain, gently curved wall with entrances at both ends (see page 47).

Attempts to provide accommodation by screening off parts of the church with solid partitions are generally less successful. The traditional box-like panelled vestry with a square top, crouching in the

St Nicholas, Warwick, Coventry Diocese: (top) new sanctuary in eastern part of the nave; (bottom) meeting room in upper part of the former chancel.

corner of aisle or nave, has always seemed visually unintegrated, but remains a pattern still sometimes followed. It is preferable to use a simple rail and curtain, which at least betrays the temporary nature of the arrangement. More successful are full-height solid screens, provided they are sited on the lines of arcades or existing openings.

There have been a number of schemes for the construction of new rooms or entrance foyers at the west end of the nave. At their simplest these are to provide draught lobbies. At St Marie's Roman Catholic Church, Derby, Pugin's first large church, a minimalist plate-glass screen and doors – more glass than wall – has been placed across the tower arch (c.1989). Despite elegant detailing, the lack of a metal framework and reflections on the glass create a visual barrier which interrupts the view from the west door. A more substantial solution is that at St Catherine, Gloucester, where a sizeable room has been created at the west end with gallery over (1992). The new wall across the nave has three bold arches, echoing the tripartite doors beyond. At a closer view, the top of the new wall cuts into the sight-line of the base of the west window above, but in such a generous volume and with the assured scale and detailing of the new work, the addition fits into the old.

West towers have been adapted successfully to increase accommodation and to provide required facilities. Where the west door is no longer used for access, the base of the tower has often been subdivided to provide lavatory or kitchen accommodation, although blocking the west door may create difficulties in the future. The insertion of new floors in a tower will free up the space below and, depending on the ease of access, can provide usable space above. At St Peter, Coughton, Warwickshire (1991) a new upper floor with oak balustrade provides a raised ringing chamber, open to the nave, bringing a theatrical immediacy between the ringers and the congregation (see opposite).

Where porches are sufficiently spacious, upper spaces can be created, or recreated as at St Mary, Thornbury, between Bristol and

46

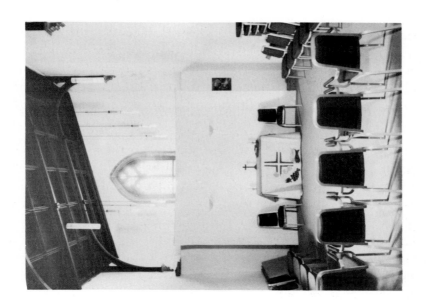

Top: St Matthew, Salford Priors, Coventry Diocese: meeting room/chapel, with kitchen behind. Bottom: St Peter, Coughton, Coventry Diocese: gallery for ringing chamber with meeting area below.

St Thomas, Huddersfield, Wakefield Diocese: (top) new sanctuary under chancel arch; (bottom) view W to gallery with meeting rooms below.

Gloucester (1992), where the Parvise Room is accessible by the original spiral stair and the new stitched discreetly into the old.

Radical rearrangement

More radical responses are sometimes called for, particularly in urban areas of social deprivation. A bold refashioning has been carried out at St Thomas, Huddersfield, (1990) where a fine, though not outstanding building by G G Scott of 1858-9 was threatened by the disappearance of its original parish of factories and terraced housing. Nearly all the earlier furnishings have been removed and replaced by a carefully designed stone font and altar. Parish rooms have been placed in the west end, with a gallery above. The new west wall and gallery balustrade have been strongly and positively modelled. An adaptable contemporary space has been created without destroying the integrity of the historic structure (see opposite).

A similarly courageous scheme was carried out at Holy Innocents, Fallowfield, Manchester (c.1990), of much the same date but by less interesting architects, Price and Linklater (illustrated overleaf). Here two parishes were combined into a single church. By turning the orientation of the building completely around and placing the new altar against the west wall, a new immediacy of worship was achieved. The smaller spaces at the east end, including the sanctuary, were converted to a meeting room, with kitchen and lavatories in the old vestry area. The end bay of the nave and aisles had a new gallery placed above, with the displaced vestry and parish office site below. Despite the importation of a splendid large cross by W D Caröe as a focus at the west end, the interior contains fewer architectural pleasures than at St Thomas. However both these projects illustrate how parishes with all the associated social problems of urban life can transcend financial and physical difficulties and carry substantial schemes through to completion.

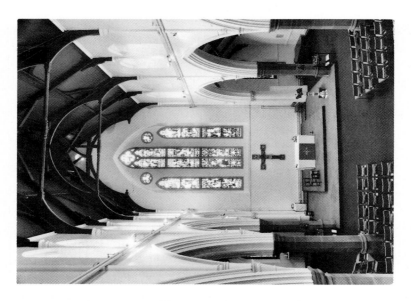

Holy Innocents, Fallowfield, Manchester Diocese: (top) new sanctuary at W end of nave; (bottom) gallery and meeting rooms in former chancel.

Even greater social problems at St Matthew, Nechells, Birmingham (1992) have resulted in proposals for making a Resource Centre for the City Social Services with space for community offices out of William Thomas's 1840 church, and leaving a much reduced worship area at the east end. Nechells is one of the most deprived districts in the Birmingham conurbation and the scheme is a partnership between the church and local and central government. The space for worship is contained within the three eastern bays and shallow chancel of the original church, with narrow first floor galleries using the old balcony fronts. This preserves something of the original, but the remaining four bays of the nave to the west are subdivided with two new floors above containing office space, which spills over into the west tower. At ground floor level the church area is still approached through the west door and the usual facilities are provided. The radical alterations mean that much will be lost but, even setting aside the important community benefits of the project, it will allow the preservation of the majority of the exterior and of something of the interior, which must surely be preferable to dereliction and eventual demolition.

External extensions

The topic of church extensions provokes an instant and hostile reception from conservationists. Whilst, as will already be clear, extensions must be regarded as the least satisfactory way of providing new accommodation, there is nothing new about such proposals. The typical medieval parish church has changed greatly over the centuries to meet altered needs within the parish. This has applied as much to the outside of the church as the inside. Aisles have been added, nave walls removed, towers and transepts built on and chancels rebuilt. The building form of the average parish church is a record of organic and accumulated growth and removal. We are perhaps more conscious of the alteration work of the nine-teenth century, a period that is only now becoming fully appreciated again, but it would be wrong to think that the Victorians did more than any other age to remodel our churches. What has changed is that we appear to lack confidence in the work for which we ourselves are responsible. The negative approach to church adaptation and extension that is reflected in recent publications is clearly founded on a feeling of acute embarrassment and concern at the disappointing quality of so much that has been built.

As has been suggested above, there are certain basic considerations to be taken into account when contemplating extensions to churches. Other ways should first be investigated to provide what is needed. But, if an extension proves to be the only answer, careful consideration should be given to the siting of the extension, the scale and form of it, the materials and the architectural treatment and detail. As has been mentioned earlier, a careful historical and physical analysis should be conducted by the parish and its architect to gain a closer understanding of how the building has developed over the centuries, and to investigate the spaces and volumes available within the existing fabric.

Siting is important in minimising the visual impact of new extensions. For this reason the north side of the church is often preferred. However the new accommodation must be arranged in a way that makes sense not only of the churchyard but of the overall building in use. The link between new and old can be critical. Significant removal of medieval or important later work cannot be countenanced in the context of a proper care for the integrity and archaeology of the existing structure. Thus, where extensions are attached and parallel with the church, it is important to preserve the original outer wall. A narrow glazed link between the old and new is often proposed in order to minimise structural disturbance. However this solution has received much condemnation, partly because it can create a sunless and weed-filled gap between old and new, and partly because it forms such a weak connection visually, so that the new work seems semi-detached, rather than successfully integrated into the whole.

Both English Heritage and the Society for the Protection of Ancient Buildings advocate keeping any new work subservient to the existing but there is growing concern that, as has been discussed above, such an emphasis can create an unsatisfactory imbalance between new and old. While the height of new extensions needs to relate to their intended function, it is important for the new work to be of sufficient scale to allow it to sit comfortably next to the old. As with the detailed design, a proper degree of confidence and assurance is essential to ensure a successful relationship. The form of new work should be allowed to grow naturally out of a study of the old.

Traditional building forms were governed by the limitations of their technology and the local availability of materials. In general this resulted in rectangular buildings, with modest roof spans and uncomplicated pitched roof forms. The modern 'chapter house' design of an octagon, so often proposed for church extensions, is usually alien to the character of what is there, and implies inappropriate aspiration to grandeur. It has been condemned for being difficult to use and almost impossible to extend.

As with internal work, the nature and quality of the materials chosen are critical to success. Materials must, in SPAB's apt phrase, do 'honour to the original'. To compromise by producing an over-economic specification will leave the new work looking inadequate and second-rate by contrast with the old.

In the examples that follow it will be apparent how the success of a scheme will hinge on the abilities of the designer. Quality in design can be simply stated and does not necessarily require a significantly increased budget. The enjoyment of past ages, their evident pride in working on God's house, are clear in the visual pleasure of their work. Very often it is the approach to small details that gives a building its overall quality and delight. New work on old churches should strive to emulate this standard. Better not to build at all, than to produce something of an unacceptable standard.

Top: St Mary, Prestbury, Gloucester Diocese: extension to vestry on N side.
Bottom: St Lawrence, Bradwell, Oxford Diocese: extension to N of W tower.

At All Saints, Stock, Essex, an extension was provided parallel with the north aisle (illustrated on the front cover). The plan is a simple rectangle, the pitched roof form echoes that of the aisle and the materials also match the original. The window forms would perhaps offend English Heritage by their 'ecclesiastical pedigree', but the whole is neat and fits in unobtrusively. It illustrates perfectly the points made in the Essex County Council/Chelmsford DAC guide. At St Mary, Prestbury, Gloucestershire (1989) remodelling and extension were concentrated on the Victorian vestry on the north side, which was widened to provide sufficient space for a new vestry and upper room. The dark-stained wooden boarding, a pitched roof and matching stonework make it clear to the observer that the work is modern but it still seems a perfectly natural development of the original building. Access to the new was here provided by moving the organ to the west end and hanging it ingeniously and dramatically from the roof (see opposite). At St Lawrence, Bradwell, now part of Milton Keynes (1992) a neat northern extension has been contrived to provide a small meeting room, vestry, etc. An unusual feature here is that the link is provided by a north door in the tower, thereby leaving the rest of the building unencumbered (see opposite). Whilst the scheme is a direct and sensitive response to the character and materials of the original, this is clearly a modern construction and the fenestration is appropriate but not pastiche-medieval.

On a larger scale, at St Mary, Lawford, Essex (1992) a new 'T' shaped wing was built out from the Georgian north aisle to provide a church hall, vestry, lavatories and kitchen for a growing population (illustrated on page 57). The scale and materials of the new work are positively handled and the overall effect adds interest to the original. At All Saints, Harbury, Warwickshire (1988) an excellent new parish room was built on the north west corner with a two-bay link to the north aisle. Access is via the old north door and none of the original fabric was removed. The extension is plain brick to match the tower material beneath a pitched clay tile roof and sited so that the new building is almost concealed (see overleaf).

55

All Saints, Harbury, Coventry Diocese: extension to N of N aisle.

The south is traditionally the most open and therefore the most cherished view of the parish church. Any intrusion is therefore likely to be a problem. An example of how things can easily go wrong is the extension to the south at St Mary the Virgin, Great Bentley, Essex (1987). Apparently there was little choice, but this extension could scarcely have been placed in a more unfortunate position. It obstructs the open view of the church from the south and conceals an attractive Norman doorway. The materials, particularly the roof tiles and white painted joinery, are inappropriate. That the extension was built at all was a remarkable achievement, much of it being constructed by the direct labour of the parishioners themselves. Although the scheme satisfied both the ecclesiastical and secular system of control, the result detracts significantly from the original building.

Extending at the west end is similarly sensitive. Very often the west front has been contrived or has evolved as the principal entrance.

St Mary, Lawford, Chelmsford Diocese: (top) 'T'-shaped extension to N of N aisle, from the E; (bottom) interior of hall in extension from the W.

Any addition here can destroy the coherence of the overall architectural composition. An illustration of this was the first scheme for Emmanuel, Loughborough, Leicestershire where a single-storey extension, of the same width, area and axis as the nave, was to be placed at the west end to provide a large hall, vestries and generous facilities for an expanding and lively urban church. The original front of 1835-7 by Thomas Rickman was simple and restrained, with Gothic used as applied ornament; it would have been cut off at the knees by the proposed extension. A revised scheme (1993) placed a substantial extension along the north side with the new building brought forward of the west front to create a sense of an enclosed forecourt, leaving the west end unencumbered. An unusual example of west end development, illustrating how rules can be broken successfully, is the new 'exo-narthex' at St Andrew, Linton Road, Oxford (1988-89), see opposite. Here the architect has skilfully extracted and reinterpreted the essence and intentions of the basilican design by A R G Fenning of 1906, placing the usual parish rooms and facilities across the west end, in such a way as to highlight the qualities of the original building.

Very occasionally the scale and nature of a problem will prove sufficiently unusual for the normal rules to be set aside. The rebuilding of Brentwood Roman Catholic Cathedral is illustrative of the sort demanded. Strictly in terms of care and conservation of the original 1861 building (by Burles Newton and Partners) and of the interesting 1974 extension, the scheme is to be condemned. The extension is twice as large as the original church. The north wall and aisle have been swept away and the church re-oriented with the first nave becoming a form of chapel to the south. But the self-assurance of the classical extension is such that a building of undoubted quality has emerged; quite different and not to everyone's taste, but stimulating. Another less controversial scheme was similar in concept but very different in result. At St Mary, Barnes (1983), the reasons for substantial alteration and extension were less questionable; the medieval church had been largely destroyed by fire,

St Andrew, Oxford, Oxford Diocese: extension across W end with porch and meeting room.

leaving little standing apart from a tower and the south and east walls of the south aisle and the east end of the north chapel. The alterations thus amounted to substantial reconstruction but there are lessons here for any work of alteration and extension. What was left was carefully and expertly conserved. Various schemes were considered for the new building, all conceived without embarrassment and in Lethaby's spirit of being 'frankly modern'. As at Brentwood, the axis of the church was shifted from east/west to north/south. Much use is made externally of stained hardwood in the new joinery but the remaining materials tie in with the original building and the quality and confidence of the design, both within and without, are such as to give cohesion and sense to the whole. This surely is a good example of how modern design, if handled well and with sensitivity, can give visual pleasure as great as the work of past ages.

William Hawkes has been chairman of the Coventry DAC from 1986 and a member of the Council for the Care of Churches from 1990. He is a partner in the architectural firm William Hawkes/Cave-Brown-Cave, and a member of the Executive Committee of the Georgian Group.

Further reading

Chelmsford DAC and Essex County Council, *So You Want to Extend Your Church? Guidelines for Extensions to and Buildings in the Curtilage of Historic Churches,* 1990

Church Building magazine, published bi-monthly, illustrates church projects large or small, including new building, restoration and furnishing, churches, parish halls and schools. It is inter-denominational and covers buildings of other faiths in the UK and abroad.

Council for the Care of Churches/Church House Publishing, *The Churchyards Handbook,* revised edition 1988

Council for the Care of Churches/Church House Publishing, *Mission in Mortar: the Role of the Church Building in the Decade of Evangelism,* 1993

Council for the Care of Churches/Church House Publishing, *Heating Your Church,* revised edition 1996

Council for the Care of Churches/Church House Publishing, *Lighting of Churches,* revised edition 1996

Council for the Care of Churches/Church House Publishing, *Wiring of Churches,* revised edition 1996

Council for the Care of Churches, *Churchscape* (annual journal)

English Heritage, *New Work in Historic Churches,* 1991

English Heritage, *Insuring Your Historic Building: Churches and Chapels,* 1994

English Heritage, *Easy Access to Historic Properties,* 1995

General Synod of the Church of England, *Care of Churches and Ecclesiastical Jurisdiction Measure: Code of Practice,* 1993

Rochester Diocese, *Reframing the Questions: a guide to the reordering of existing churches and the building of new,* edited by Derek Phillips, 1990

Society for the Protection of Ancient Buildings, *Church Extensions,* 1991

Useful addresses

Ancient Monuments Society
St Ann's Vestry Hall
2 Church Entry
London EC4V 5HB
Tel: 0171 236 3934
Fax: 0171 329 3677

Church and Community Trust
Napier Hall
Hide Place
London SW1P 4NJ
Tel and fax: 0171 976 6347

Churches Main Committee
Fielden House
Little College Street
London SW1P 3SH
Tel: 0171 222 4984
Fax: 0171 233 1104

Council for British Archaeology
Bowes Morrell House
111 Walmgate
York YO1 2UA
Tel: 01904 671417
Fax: 01904 671384

Council for the Care of Churches
Fielden House
Little College Street
London SW1P 3SH
Tel: 0171 222 3793
Fax: 0171 222 3794

Ecclesiastical Architects' and
    Surveyors' Association
Scan House
29 Radnor Cliff
Folkestone
Kent
CT20 2JJ
Tel: 01303 254008
Fax: 01227 450964

English Heritage
23 Savile Row
London W1X 1AB
Tel: 0171 973 3000
Fax: 0171 973 3001

Georgian Group
6 Fitzroy Square
London W1P 6DX
Tel: 0171 387 1720
Fax: 0171 387 1721

Royal Commission on Historical
    Monuments (England)
National Monuments Record
    Centre
Kemble Drive
Swindon
Wiltshire SN2 2GZ
Tel: 01793 414625
Fax: 01793 414771

Royal Institute of British
  Architects
66 Portland Place
London W1N 4AD
Tel: 0171 580 5533
Fax: 0171 255 1541

Royal Institute of Chartered
  Surveyors
12 Great George Street
Parliament Square
London SW1P 3AD
Tel: 0171 222 7000
Fax: 0171 222 9430

Society for the Protection of
  Ancient Buildings
37 Spital Square
London E1 6DY
Tel: 0171 377 1644
Fax: 0171 247 5296

Twentieth Century Society
70 Cowcross Street
London EC1M 6BP
Fax: 0171 250 3857
Fax: 0171 250 3022

Victorian Society
1 Priory Gardens
Bedford Park
London W4 1TT
Tel: 0181 994 1019
Fax: 0181 995 4895

Except the Lord build the house,
their labour is but lost that built it.

Psalm 127.1